Content

Check Your Mail

People all around the world send letters, postcards, and packages to their friends and family.

They mail them at a post office, or put them into a street mailbox. Then postal workers collect, sort, and deliver them. The last step in a letter's journey is when you go to your letter box to check your mail!

Mailboxes come in many shapes and sizes.

1

Send the mail

2

Collect the mail

3

Sort the mail

4

Deliver the mail

5

Check your mail

3

April 24

Dear Tomika,

This is the beach near our house. Today I went for a swim. It was very warm and I saw lots of colourful fish.

See you,
Matt

PS Write back soon!

Tomika Milas
35 Coventry Lane
London, SL6 2QR
UK

May 2

Dear Matt,

This is a famous clock called Big Ben. There are many buildings and bridges in the city where I live. I like Big Ben the best.

Bye for now,
Tomika

PS Write back again soon!

Matt Ryan

5 Wallaroo Road

Brisbane, QL 3680

Australia

London
May
3
Post Office

London

20p

5

From: Matt Ryan

Sent: Wednesday, May 4, 7:15 A.M.
To: Tomika Milas
Subject: Sun, Sea, and Surf!

Dear Tomika,

This is my first e-mail. I only got my computer yesterday. Mum helped me send this picture. Open it and see what my sister and I look like.

Your e-pal,
Matt

MATT.jpg

MATT.jpg

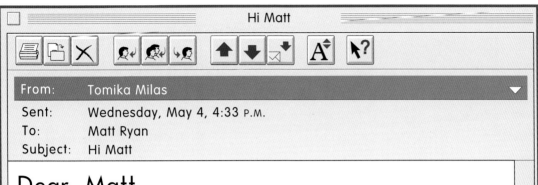

From: Tomika Milas

Sent: Wednesday, May 4, 4:33 P.M.
To: Matt Ryan
Subject: Hi Matt

Dear Matt,

I got your e-mail. I liked your picture. I would love to see the beach by your house. I have sent you a picture of my family. I am on the right.

Bye,
Tomika

ME.jpg

7

Jacko the Junk Shop Man

Written by Margaret Mahy
Illustrated by Jo Davies

Jade was reading her alphabet book.
"I feel sorry for the letter **j**,"
she said.

"Why?" asked her mother.

"Because **b** has lots of words, **g** has
lots of words, but **j** hasn't got many
words at all. Poor **j**!" said Jade.

"Ah," replied her mother. "Let me tell
you about Jacko the junk shop man!"

9

Jacko the junk shop man enjoyed his junk. "I wish I had someone to enjoy this junk with me," he said.

Jubilee, his jolly wife,
made lots of jokes. She also made
lots of jam and jelly.
"I wish we had visitors to help us
eat our jam and jelly," she said.

One day, Jacko said, "I'm up early.
I'll go jogging around town."
Jacko put on his jacket.

Jog,

jog,

jog.

Jacko jogged
by the dance hall.
He met a jazz band.
"The wheel has come
off our bus," they cried.
"It's so cold in the snow."

12

Jacko said, "Jog along,
jog along, jog through the snow.
Jogging will soon make you warm,
you know!"

As they jogged along, they met
a high jumper and a long jumper
and a man with a javelin.
Jacko said, "High jumper, long jumper,
it's cold, but don't fuss!
Javelin thrower, come jogging with us."

They jogged by the jetty and
met a pirate with a trunk of jewels.
His name was Jumbo Jink.
He was lost and very cold.

But Jacko said, "Jog along, Jumbo,
jog along with me, we're all going home
for a cup of tea."

Off they went, jogging and jogging, past the jungle at the edge of town. Then out jumped a jaguar.

"A jaguar!" cried the javelin thrower, about to throw his javelin.

Jacko stopped him and said,
"Joggers are gentle with jaguars, too.
Jog along, jaguar, jog along do.
Jog along, jaguar. Jog along all.
Jubilee's joyful when visitors call."

17

Jubilee looked out of the window
and saw them jogging through the gate.
"We'll have a jam roll, a jug of juice,
jelly, and jelly beans!" she cried.
"And we'll have them in a jiffy."

Everyone crowded into the junk shop.
"We'll soon have this joint jumping,"
cried the jazz men.

The jumpers jumped high and long over the junk. Jumbo Jink gave Jubilee a jewel. And the javelin thrower and the jaguar became good friends.

"Oh, thank you, Mum," said Jade.
"The letter **j** is very grateful to you.
Tomorrow you can do **z**!"

Secrets
of a
Storyteller

Introducing Margaret Mahy

Born: New Zealand

Interests: Playing with her cat, walking her dog, playing games, and singing with her grandchildren

Favourite Stories: Scary, funny, or family stories

Q: What did you write about when
you were a child?

A: When I was eight or nine, all the stories
I wrote were about wild horses.
When I wrote them, it almost seemed
as if I had turned into a horse myself.

Q: Do your friends and family give
you story ideas?

A: Yes, all the time, but they don't
always know it. The ideas come out of
the unexpected things in ordinary life.

Q: Why do you enjoy storytelling?

A: I like the sound of words. I like
hearing words set free in the air around me.

Grandpa Knits

Grandpa likes to knit
in front of the TV.
He knits for his friends
and for his family.

He knits when he walks
his dog down the street.
He knitted the hat
and the socks on his feet.

He knits more than socks
and hats for his head.
He knitted the teddy
that sits on my bed.

The Father Who Walked on His Hands

Written by Margaret Mahy
Illustrated by Sandra Cammell

At lunch time, the children talked
about their mothers and fathers.

34

The next week,
Tom's father came to fix
the school bike shed.

Then Maria's mother came to talk
about eating healthy food. She came
in a taxi. Henry's mother drove the taxi.

Then, on Thursday, the class went
to the planetarium. It was dark.
They could see the stars.
Elsie's father told them all about stars.

On Friday, the teacher said, "We are
having a very special visitor today!"
There was a knock on the door...

In came a clown
with a bright red nose.
He walked upside down
with his big shoes
in the air.

He danced on his hands.
He did flips.
When he stood up,
his hat fell off,
and his little dog
did a dance.

Old Tools,

Here are some tools that people used long ago to get a job done. Match the old tools with the jobs people do today.

New Jobs

Supermarket worker

Writer

Singer

Computer operator

Laundromat worker

Photographer

Receptionist

41

ON HOLIDAY

Written by Josh Ryan ✷ Photographed by Andy Belcher

This was the day I'd been waiting
and waiting and **waiting** for!

We were going on holiday.
Me and my family and my best friend, Meg.

HOORAY! We are here at last.
First we unpacked the car.
Phew! That was hard work.

Next we put up the tent.
Phew! That was even harder work.

At last, it was time
to play, play, play!

45

Meg and I went swimming every day.
We jumped and splashed in the water.
We swam and swam and swam.

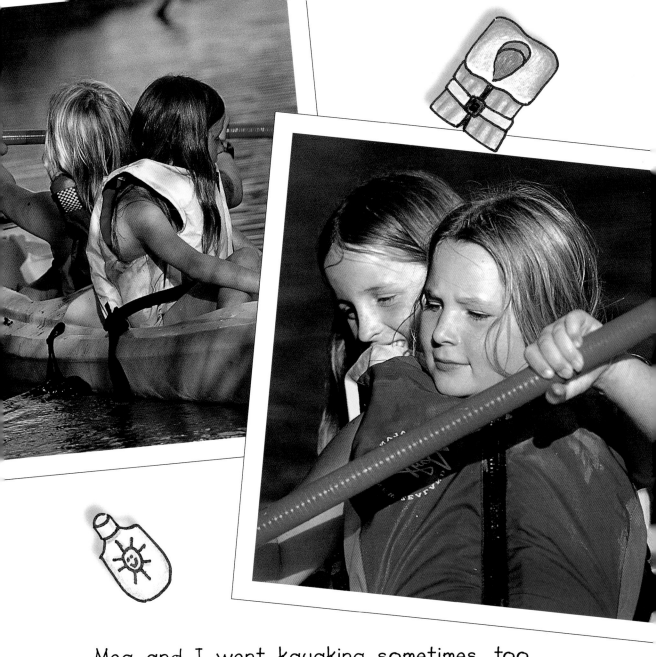

Meg and I went kayaking sometimes, too.
We looked for eels in the water.
We paddled and paddled and paddled.

47

Dad woke us up early
every morning to go fishing.

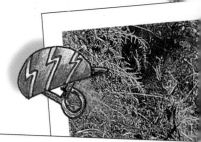

48

Sometimes we even caught a fish!

Some days we went biking.
We biked up, up, up the hills.

Some days we went hiking.
We raced down, down, down the hills.

49

At night, we cooked sausages over the campfire.

We stayed up late and told stories under the starry sky.

Being on holiday was lots of fun, but it sure did make us tired.

Meg and I think we need another holiday now!

Letters That Go Together

kn knit, knock, know

Sounds I Know

-ai	mail	**-ea**	head
-ee	feet	**-e**	bed

Beginnings I Know

-a about
      along
      around

Words I Know

about	cried	has	were
along	don't	he's	when
around	family	very	you
but	friends	we'll	your

52